This Book Belongs To

_____

If you would like to see more images and stay updated on new coloring books, visit our web page at www.selahworks.com.
Printed in the U.S.A.

Copyright © 2018 Selah Works Prints
ISBN-13: 978-1725806818
ISBN-10: 1725806819

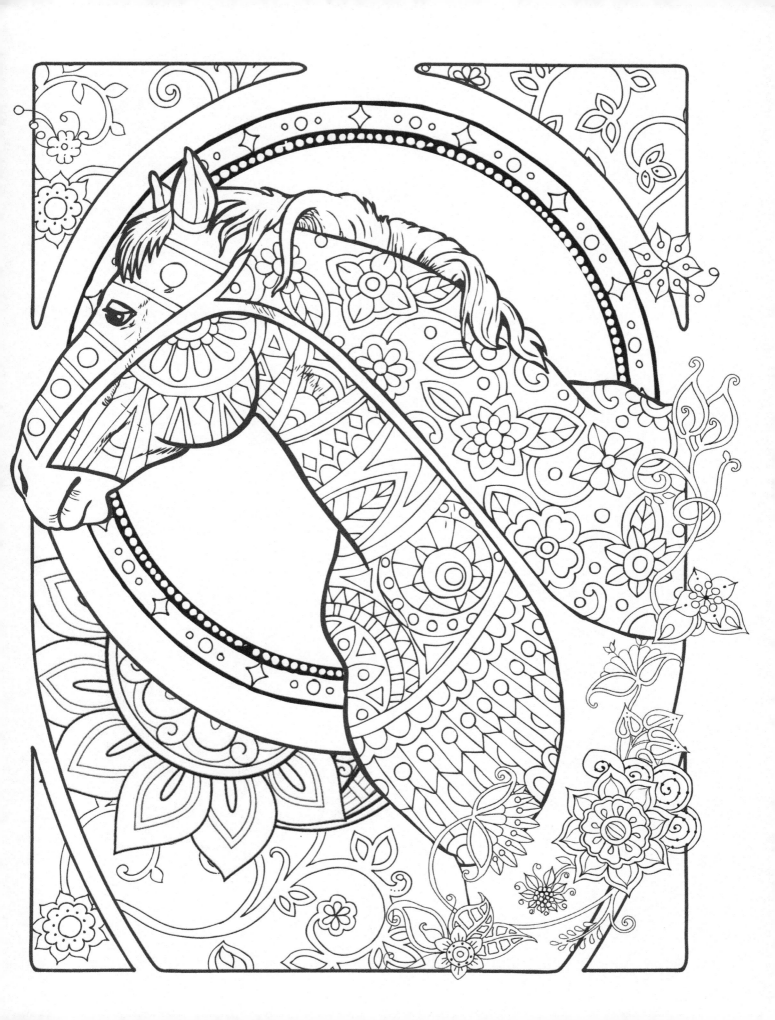

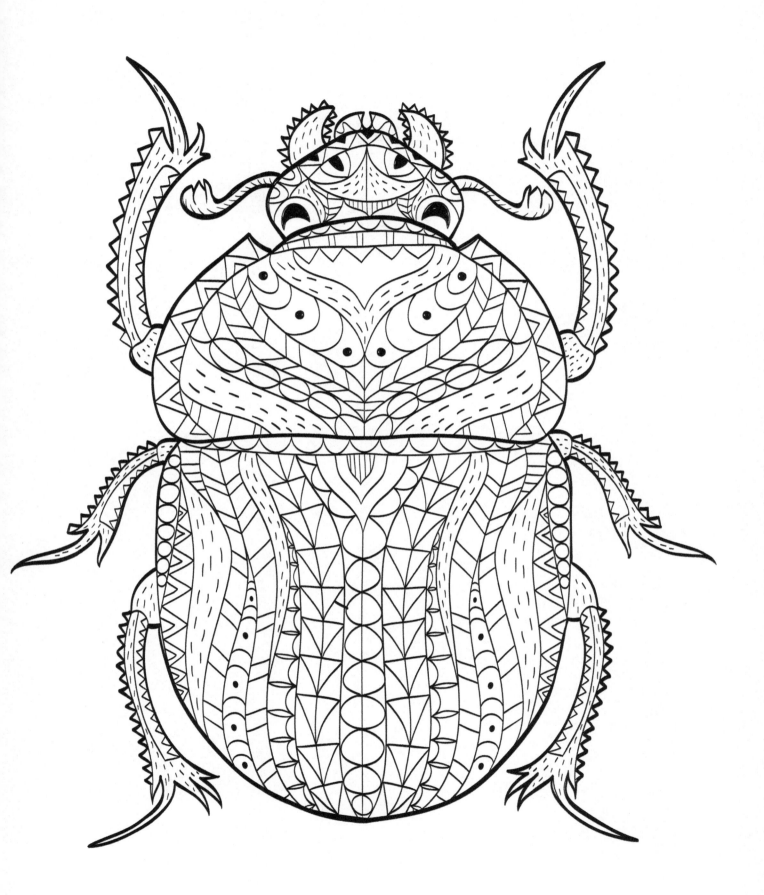

IT WOULD MEAN SO MUCH TO ME IF YOU CAN LEAVE A REVIEW AND LET OTHERS KNOW WHAT YOU THINK! GO HERE TO LEAVE A REVIEW

HTTPS://GOO.GL/COMHRT

MY GIFT TO YOU!
FREE PDF DOWNLOAD OF PAGES NOT INCLUDED IN THIS BOOK. GO HERE TO GET YOUR BONUS GIFT DOWNLOAD

HTTP://BONUSGIFT.PAGEDEMO.CO